T · H · E
QUINTESSENTIAL
·CROISSANT·

T · H · E
QUINTESSENTIAL
·CROISSANT·

PAMELLA Z. ASQUITH
Text

MICHAEL STARKMAN
Design and Illustration

CELESTIAL ARTS, Millbrae, California

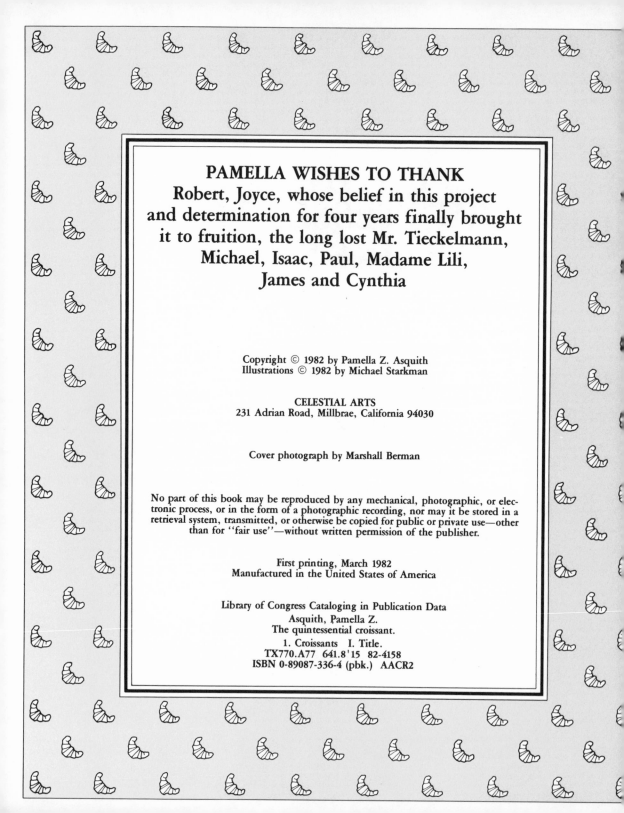

PAMELLA WISHES TO THANK
Robert, Joyce, whose belief in this project
and determination for four years finally brought
it to fruition, the long lost Mr. Tieckelmann,
Michael, Isaac, Paul, Madame Lili,
James and Cynthia

CELESTIAL ARTS
231 Adrian Road, Millbrae, California 94030

Cover photograph by Marshall Berman

First printing, March 1982
Manufactured in the United States of America

Library of Congress Cataloging in Publication Data
Asquith, Pamella Z.
The quintessential croissant.
1. Croissants I. Title.
TX770.A77 641.8'15 82-4158
ISBN 0-89087-336-4 (pbk.) AACR2

·CONTENTS·

ONCE UPON A TIME, the year 1686 to be exact, the city of Budapest was beseiged by Turks. To penetrate the city walls, the Turks endeavored to tunnel under them by night. The noise, however, was heard by bakers working at underground ovens. The bakers informed the defensive forces who ousted the aggressors. As a symbol of victory and liberation, the bakers made a pastry in the shape of a crescent, the symbol of the Ottoman Empire.

Thus was the romantic, perhaps apocryphal, origin of the pastry still enjoyed today. The French—always fascinated by new shapes for pastry—adopted and adapted the crescent shape, and so perfected the techniques of pastry-making that the only correct and polite name for this crescent-shaped pastry is the French one—crois-sant (kwah-SAHN).

Even so, the French—always lovers of aesthetic debate—never agree on the quintessence of *any* aspect of *Haute Cuisine*. Discussions regarding the proper shade of brown, degree of crispness, size, exact shape, degrees of saltiness and sweetness are never resolved. In this spirit, we present yet another treatise on this classic pastry. No doubt, many croissant lovers—French and otherwise will be incensed at the preferences herein set forth. But let the debate go on! The ordinary inspires nothing, whereas seekers of the sublime must be prepared to struggle.

11

The object of our affection is, however, becoming an endangered species. In these inflationary times, many professional bakers, rather than raise prices, choose to substitute cheaper ingredients. And, as the proper preparation of croisants is labor-intensive and their shelf-life only about two hours, croissant-baking is not very lucrative for most commercial operations.

13

Given these problems, the Quintessential Croissant may be doomed to extinction commercially—or, even worse, mediocrity and banalization. But with the publication of this slim volume, the empassioned croissant-lover is spared the sad frustration experienced by those who would long to recreate the Great Pyramids or Medieval stained glass—the secrets of *those* wonders being forever lost to history. Following the techniques and tips herein presented, the creation of the Quintessential Croissant, the chef-d'oeuvre of pastry, is now within the grasp of all.

15

· R E C I P E ·

Enough for two dozen

Allow at least 9 hours from start to finish. (You can make the dough one day and then roll it and bake it the next.)

2 tablespoons yeast
3 tablespoons sugar
¼ cup water
1½ cups half-and-half
2 teaspoons salt
5 cups flour (1 pound, 6 ounces)
1½ cups unsalted butter (12 ounces, or 3 sticks)

GLAZE:
1 egg yolk
1 tablespoon cream
—or—
1 whole egg
1 teaspoon cream, milk, or water

SUGAR GLAZE
1 tablespoon water
½ cup powdered sugar

17

·CONSIDERATIONS·

1 THE YEAST may be either dry granulated or bakers' compressed yeast.

2 THE SUGAR does not impart a sweet taste to the dough because it is consumed by the growing yeast. If a sweeter flavor is desired, increase the amount of sugar in the dough to up to 5 tablespoons or, after baking the croissants, brush them with the Sugar Glaze.

3 THE WATER should be at body temperature, about 100°F.

18

4 THE HALF-AND-HALF should be at room temperature, about 75°F.

5 THE DEGREE of saltiness is a matter of preference. This recipe adds only enough salt to ward off blandness. Salted butter contains about 1 teaspoon salt per pound; therefore, cut the salt in the recipe by ¾ teaspoon if salted butter is used.

19

6 USING the correct flour is crucial to croissant making. The flour need not be bleached. Unless one has access to a professional source, start with an "all-purpose" flour and experiment adding different amounts of "pastry" and/or "bread" flours. A good formula is: 4½ cups all-purpose flour and ½ cup gluten flour (health food stores usually carry gluten flour). The flour should not be too glutenous (gluten forms muscle-like protein fibres which give the dough structural strength) or one will get blue in the face when trying to roll the dough. Nor should the flour be too starchy or it will not have the necessary protein structure to hold layers of dough and butter. Measuring flour by weight, not volume, is highly recommended.

Although the secret of creating the Quintessential Croissant is technique—not recipe—one should be scientifically precise when measuring ingredients. If one is experimenting with flours, salt and sugar, accuracy of measurement is essential; there are sufficient paths to disaster without further tempting fate by gambling with quantities in the recipe. Reducing this recipe is not recommended; a large piece of dough is needed in order to obtain the proper elasticity when rolling.

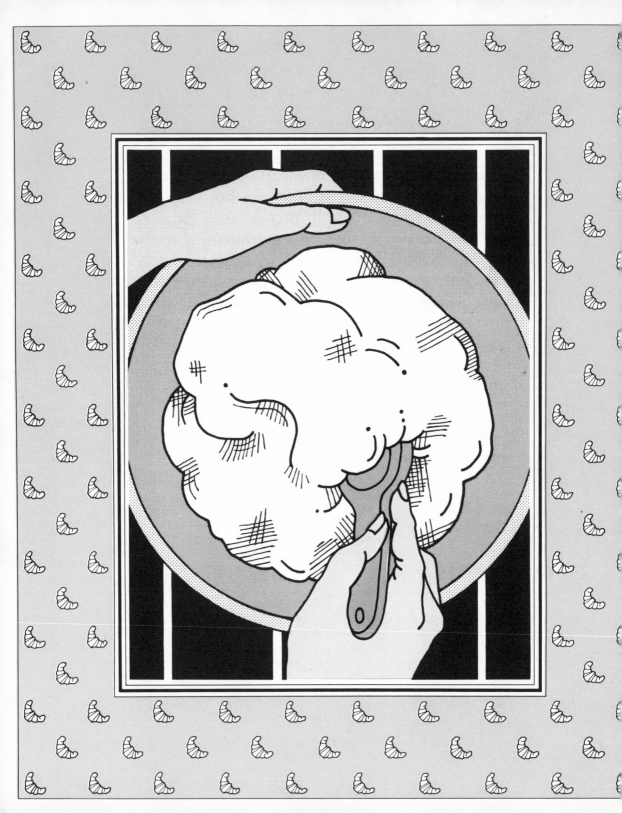

· T E C H N I Q U E ·

1 DISSOLVE the yeast and 2 tablespoons of the flour in the water. Let this mixture (*la mere* or the mama) set 10–15 minutes or until foamy.

2 POUR in the half-and-half and add sugar.

3 WORK 2½ cups of the flour into this mixture...

4 ...ADD the salt.

23

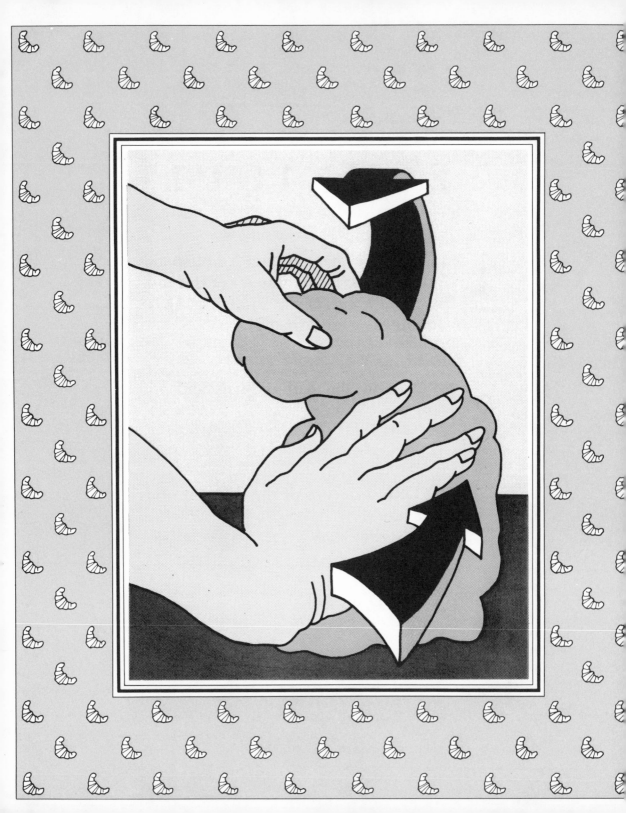

5 NOW WORK all but ¼ cup of the remaining flour into the dough (the ¼ cup is reserved for step 7). Knead only until smooth. This dough is not kneaded as thoroughly as a regular bread dough; too much kneading at this stage would make the rolling almost impossible later.

For the kneading novice: lift the edge of the dough, fold it over like an omelette, push it down with the heel of your hand, rotate it 90° and repeat.

6 PRESS the dough into a rectangle about 1 inch thick. Wrap in plastic and refrigerate 1 to 4 hours.

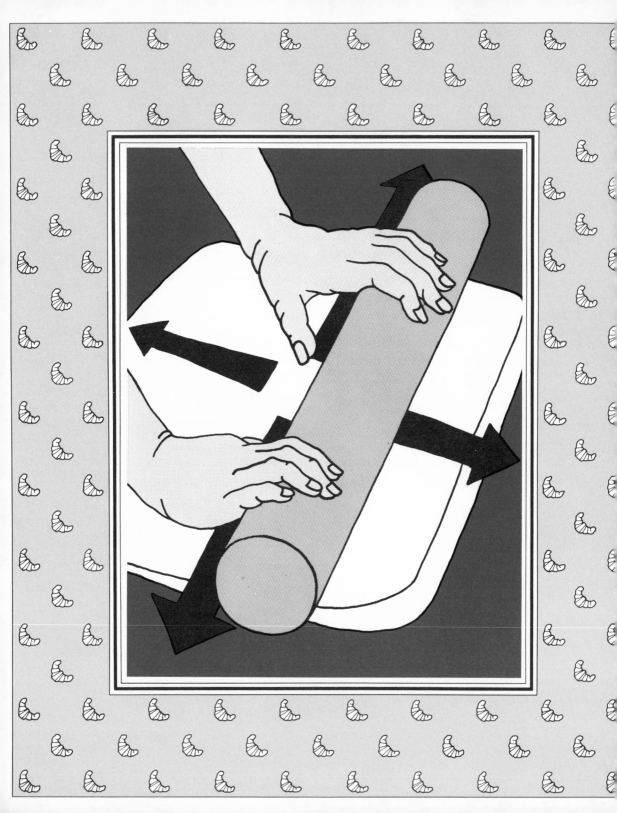

7 MIX the butter with the reserved ¼ cup flour until smooth. Press or roll the butter–flour mixture into a square approximately 10 × 10 inches, ¼ inch thick. Place it on a baking sheet and refrigerate about 15–20 minutes. The butter now should be as flexible as thick leather and should not snap when bent.

8 SPRINKLE a little flour (1 tablespoon should be sufficient; this is in addition to the 5 cups) on a pastry board at least 18 × 24 inches. *It is important that the dough and butter be about the same temperature, otherwise the butter will not form layers but pebble-like blobs.* Place the dough on the board, pound it with a rolling pin a few times to flatten it and roll it into a rectangle approximately 14 × 20 inches, ¼ inch thick. Roll from the center outwards, not back and forth, exerting pressure directly perpendicular to the dough. Flap the dough (as you would flap a beach towel to get rid of excess sand) to relax it.

27

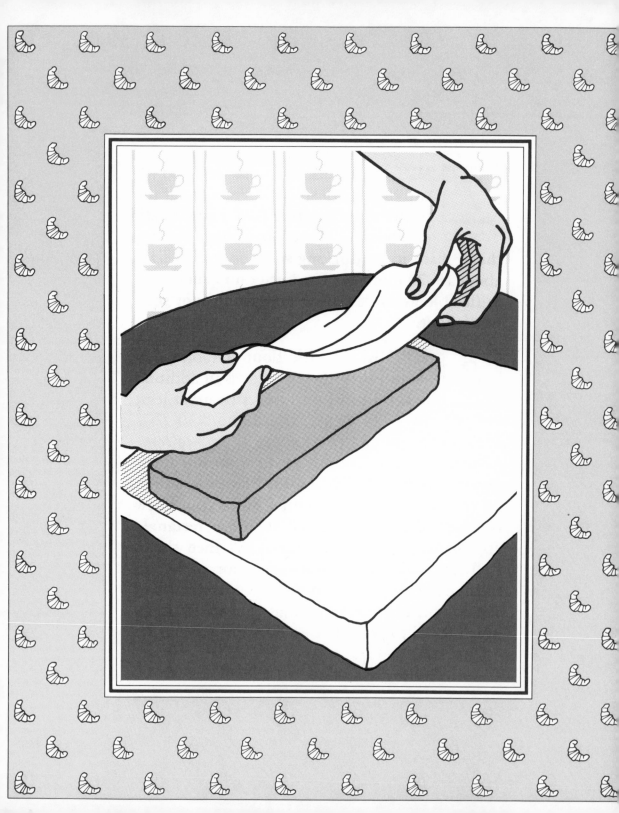

9 CUT the butter into two 5 × 10 inch pieces. Place one butter section on the center of the dough. Fold a side of the dough over the butter. Place the remaining butter on the top and fold the remaining side of the dough over it. Gently pinch the sides of the dough together. You should now have a sealed triple-decker sandwich of dough-butter-dough-butter-dough.

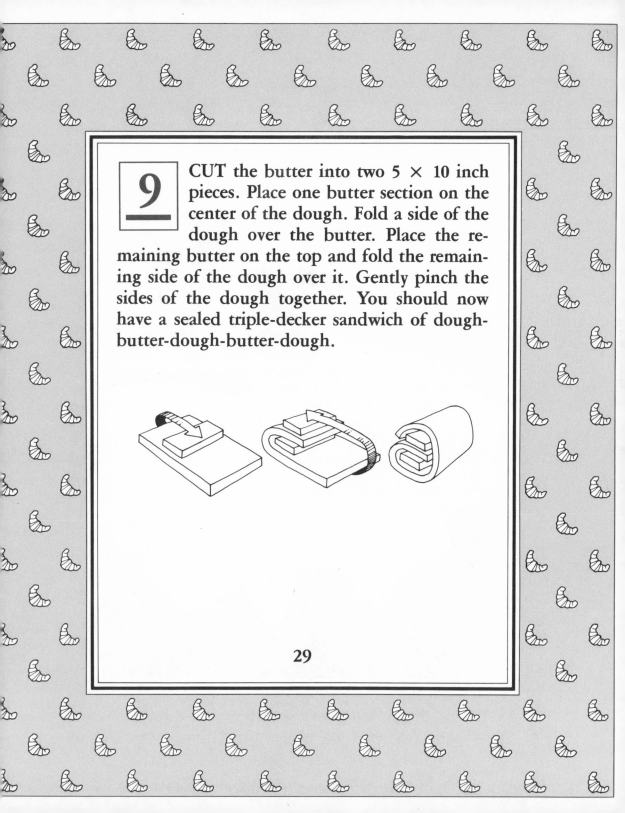

29

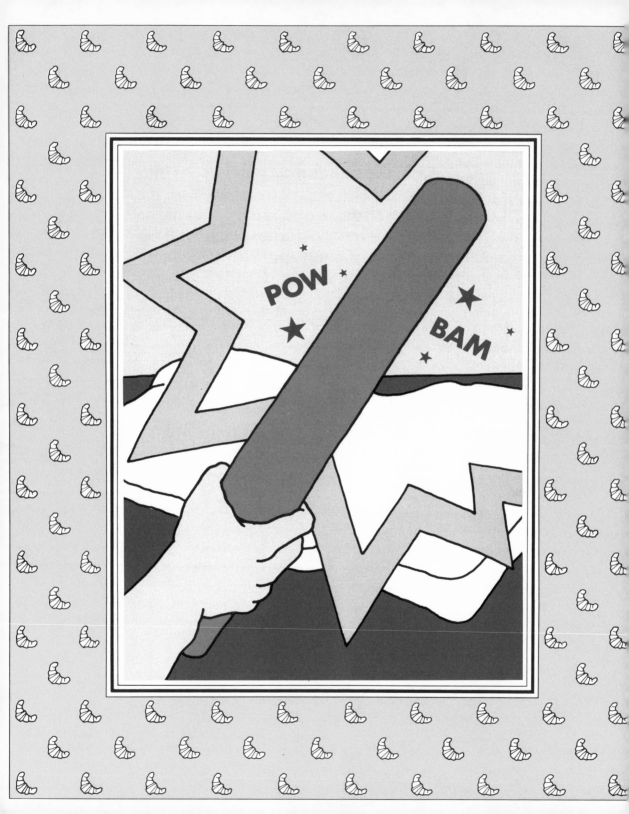

10 POUND fiercely with a rolling pin until the dough sandwich is flattened to a 1 inch thickness.

11 IF NECESSARY, SPRINKLE a little more flour (1 tablespoon should be sufficient; this is in addition to the 5 cups flour) on the pastry board (be stingy; excessive flouring will cause the dough to become tough). Roll the dough into a rectangle approximately 12 × 20 inches, ¼ inch thick. Brush away any excess flour before folding the dough. Flap the dough to relax it. Imagine the dough divided into thirds; fold the right third over the center third to form two plies, then fold the left third over the other two plies to form three plies. Gently punch the dough once with a finger. Wrap it securely in plastic and refrigerate 30 minutes to 1 hour. This time allows the dough to relax which makes it easier to roll.

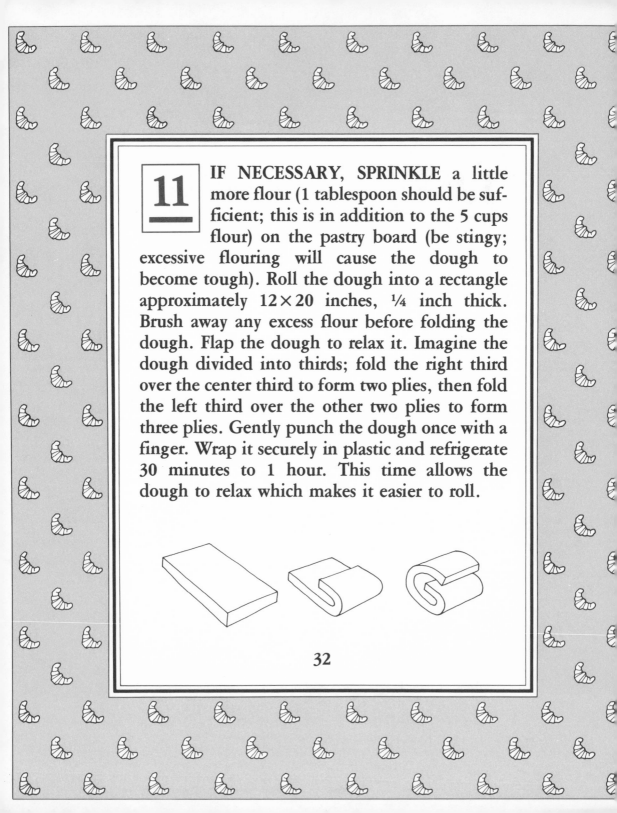

12 REPEAT step 11 five times for a total of six times. After each rolling-and-folding, gently punch the dough with a finger to indicate the total number of times you have completed this operation lest you forget. The rolling-and-folding may be done twice in a row without refrigeration in between. However, if the dough gets too difficult to roll, allow it time to relax in the refrigerator.

13 AFTER the series of rolling-and-folding has been completed, refrigerate the dough at least 4 and up to 24 hours. The dough may be frozen at this point; wrap *very* securely. (The dough must be completely thawed before you proceed to step 14).

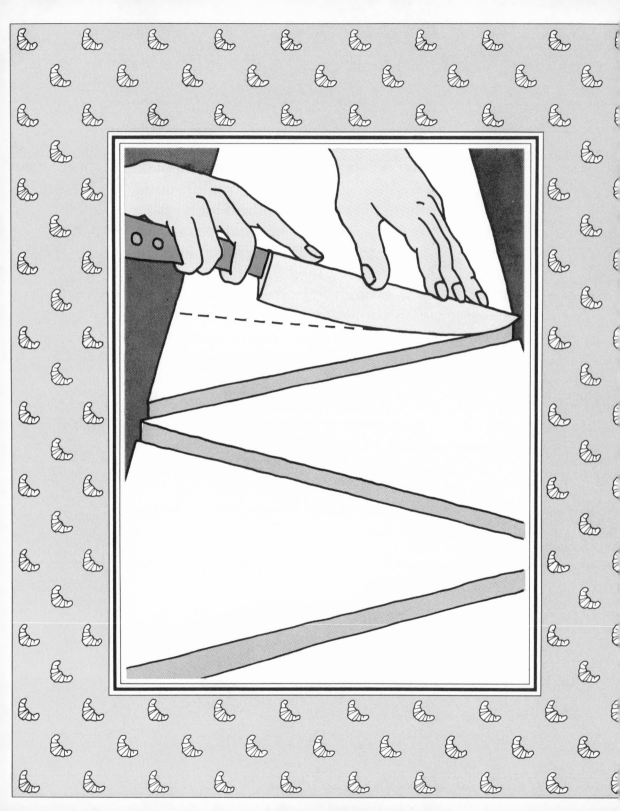

14 SPRINKLE a little flour (1 tablespoon should be sufficient; this is additional to the 5 cups) on the pastry board. Roll the dough into a rectangle approximately 13 × 21 inches, ¼ inch thick. Flap the dough to relax it.

15 WITH a sharp knife, cleaver or roll cutter, trim the dough to make the edges even and straight. Cut into two 6½ × 21 inch strips. Cut triangles 3½ inches on the short side and 6½ inches on the other 2 sides. Each triangle should weigh about 2 ounces. Do not drag the knife or cleaver or the layering effect will be destroyed. Press together 2 of the pieces at the end of each row to form another 2 triangles.

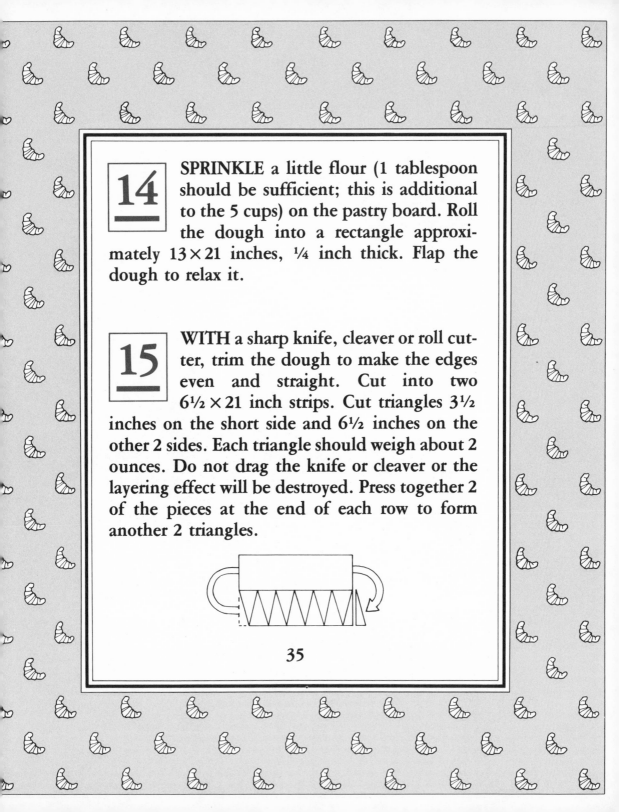

35

16

BRUSH away any excess flour and flap each triangle to relax the dough.

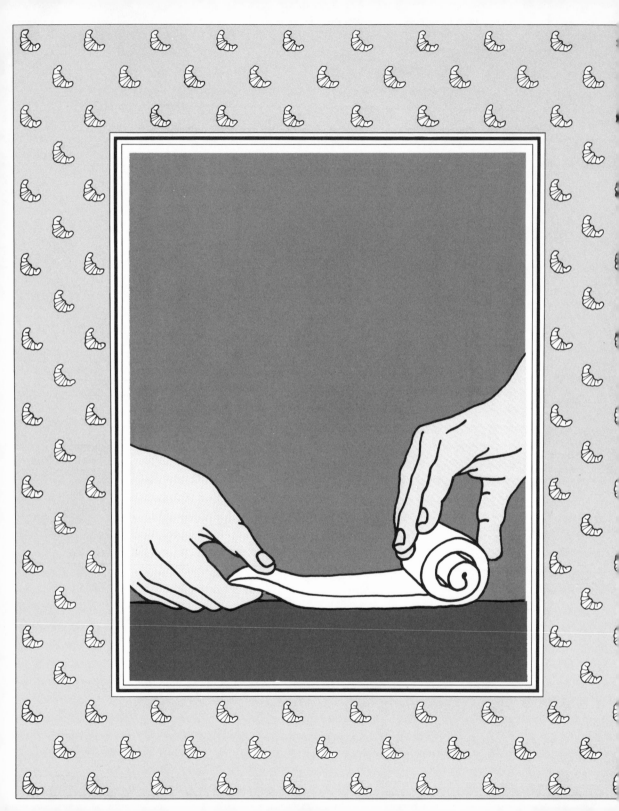

17

STARTING at the short side of the triangle, roll towards the other point. Gently stretch and pull the dough from the third corner while rolling it up.

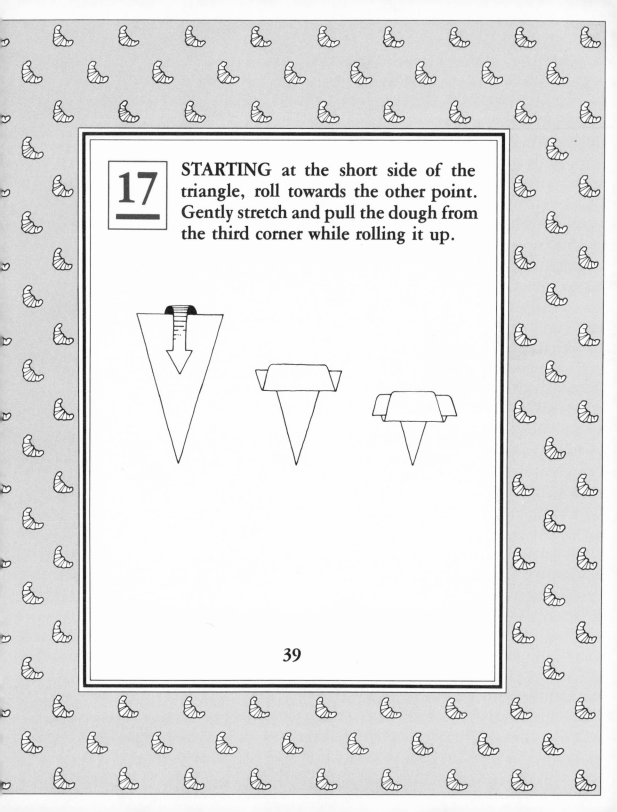

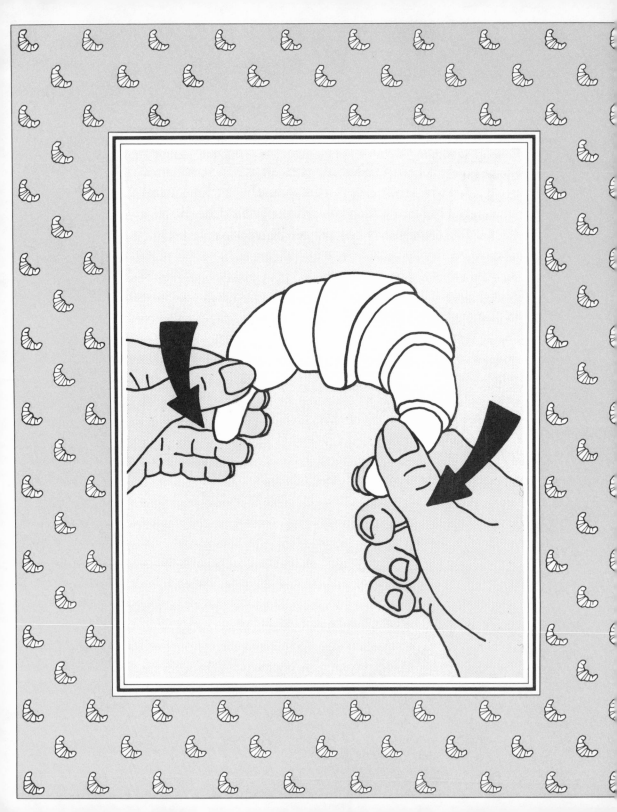

18 PLACE your thumbs in the "tails" and pull into the crescent shape. This final pull is necessary to prevent the dough from relaxing into a roly-poly "critter" shape (a "critter" is any shape not perfectly croissant-esque). The center section of the croissant should form a "V" with the point facing down. A common mistake is to pull the tails the wrong way.

19 PLACE the formed croissants 1 inch apart on a baking sheet lined with parchment or waxed paper. Cover them with a damp cloth. Allow them to rise or "proof" in a warm (100°F) place until the dough feels soft and seems to sweat. This may take from 30 minutes to 1½ hours. Spritz the formed croissants with water if necessary to prevent the dough from drying out.

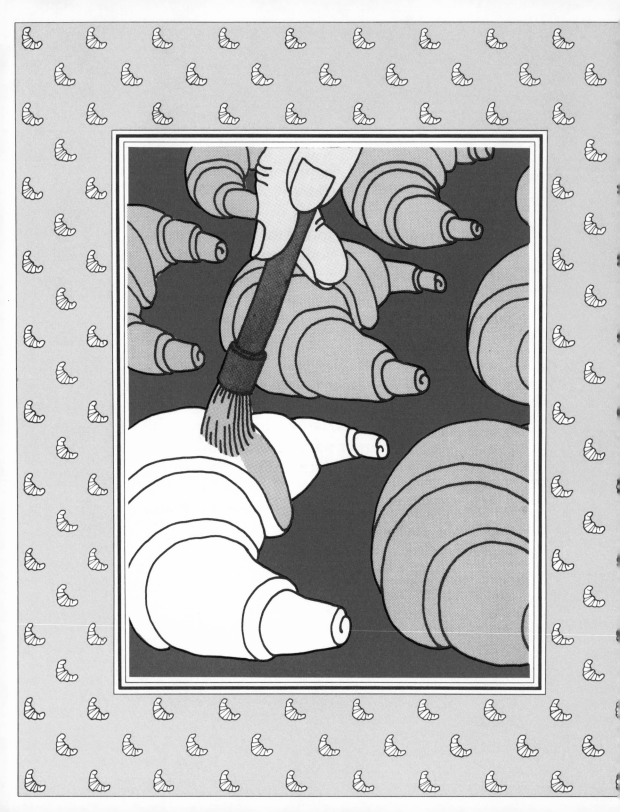

20 WHISK the egg yolk with the 1 tablespoon cream, or the whole egg with the 1 teaspoon cream, milk or water to make the glaze. Brush the egg glaze on the risen croissants. Be sparing of the glaze as too much tastes offensive.

Glaze the croissants with the basic egg glaze even if you want to sugar glaze them for additional sweetness. The sugar glaze is brushed on after baking.

21 PREHEAT your oven to 400°F. Bake the croissants until golden brown, approximately 20–25 minutes. Rotate the baking sheet if necessary to obtain even browning.

43

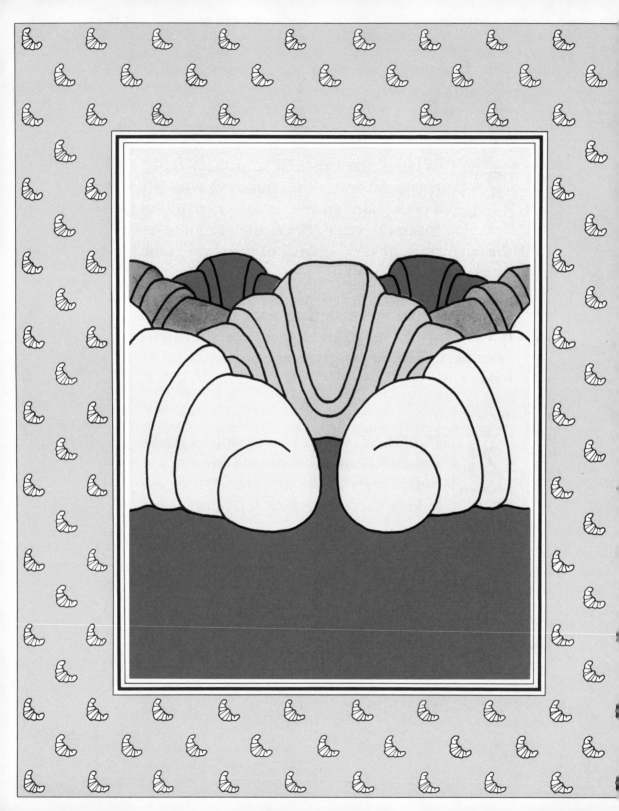

22 PLACE the baked croissants on a flat basket to cool. Croissants should be thoroughly cooled before eating. If the steam has not completely evaporated, the inside will be doughy and the croissant will seem under-baked. (Blend the 1 tablespoon water and ½ cup powdered sugar until smooth and brush it on the cooled croissants if desired.)

23 AT LAST, ingest and enjoy!

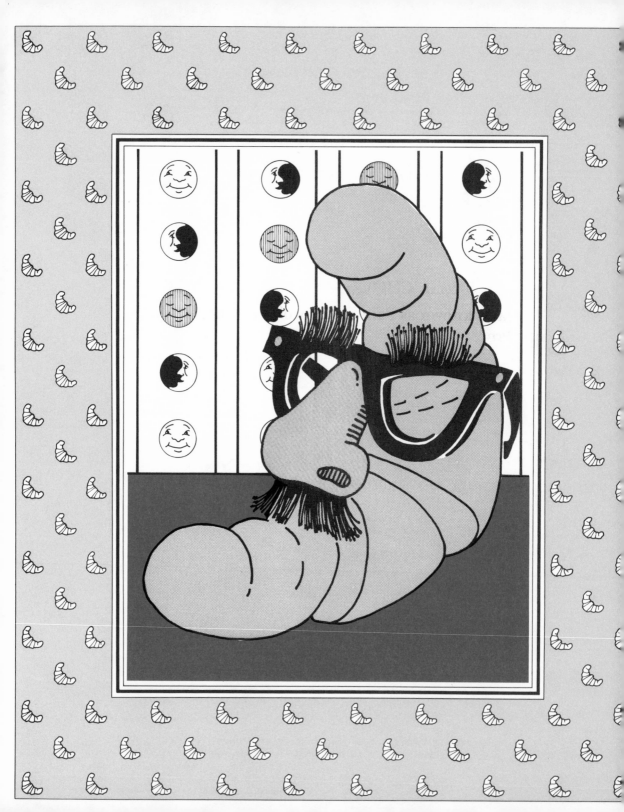

· V A R I A T I O N S ·

O N   T H E   T H E M E

THE CHOCOLATE VARIATION

(also known as Pain au Chocolat or Chocolatine)
Proceed through step 14. Divide the basic
13 × 21 inch rectangle into squares about 3 × 3
inches. Place one ounce of good bittersweet
chocolate on each square. Fold each corner on
the diagonal like an envelope and pinch to seal.
Then proceed from step 19, proof, glaze and
bake. Beware however, these confections are ad-
dicting! Witness the following...

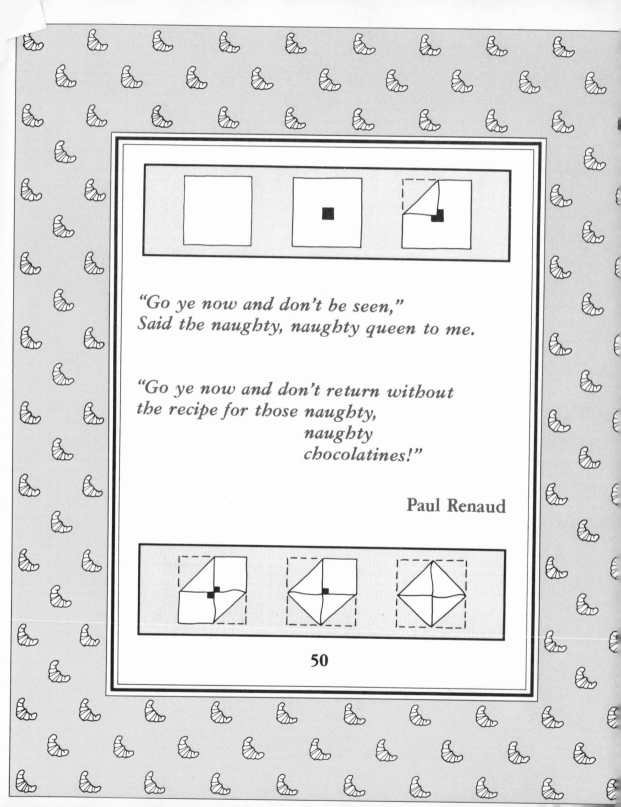

"Go ye now and don't be seen,"
Said the naughty, naughty queen to me.

"Go ye now and don't return without
the recipe for those naughty,
                    naughty
                        chocolatines!"

Paul Renaud

50

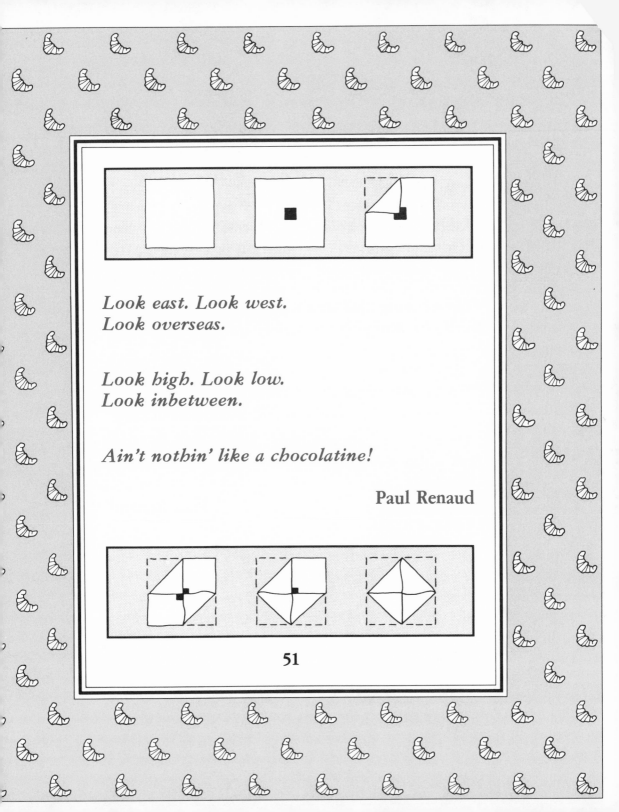

Look east. Look west.
Look overseas.

Look high. Look low.
Look inbetween.

Ain't nothin' like a chocolatine!

Paul Renaud

VARIATIONS ON THE CHOCOLATE VARIATION

Add 4 or 5 whole roasted coffee beans, your favorite liqueur filled bon-bon or candied citrus rind to a chocolatine before baking.

THE CINNAMON* VARIATION

Proceed through step 14. Spread 2 cups of brown sugar mixed with 1 teaspoon each of cinnamon and cloves over the basic 13 × 21 inch rectangle. Roll it up at the 21 inch side, cut slices 1 inch thick and place them in buttered muffin tins. Proceed from step 19, proof, glaze and bake.

* One stands warned never to serve this variation to a French person, as the use of cinnamon in cooking is virtually grounds for divorce in France. The French take pride in the fact that the only thing their rats did not eat during the war was cinnamon.

THE FRUIT VARIATION

Proceed through step 14. Divide the basic 13 × 21 inch rectangle into squares about 4 × 4 inches. Place ¼ cup of apple, apricot, fig, prune or raisin filling on each square. Fold over on the diagonal and pinch to seal. Proceed from step 19, proof, glaze and bake.

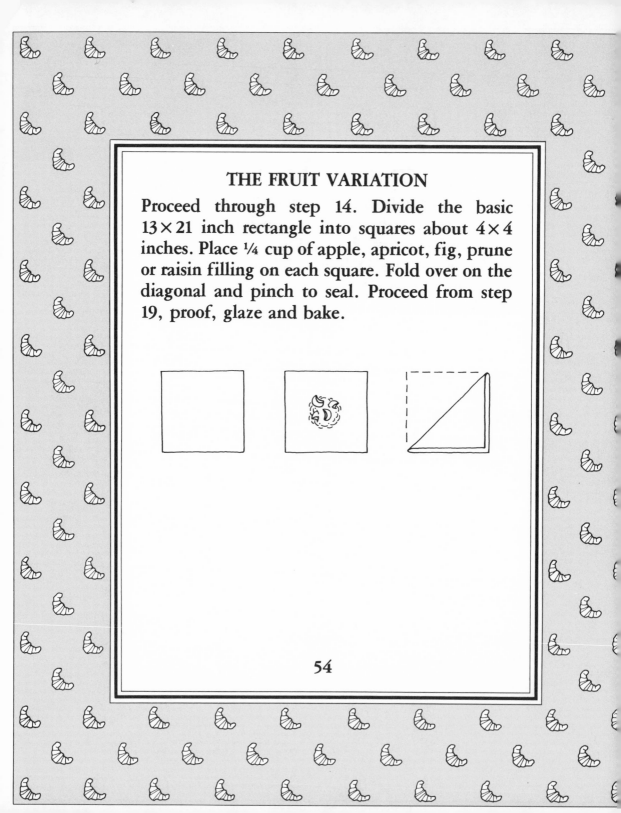

THE NUT VARIATION

Proceed through step 14. Spread 2 cups of frangipane or any ground nut filling over the basic 13 × 21 inch rectangle. Roll it up at the 21 inch side, cut slices 1 inch thick and place them in buttered muffin tins. Proceed from step 19, proof, glaze and bake.

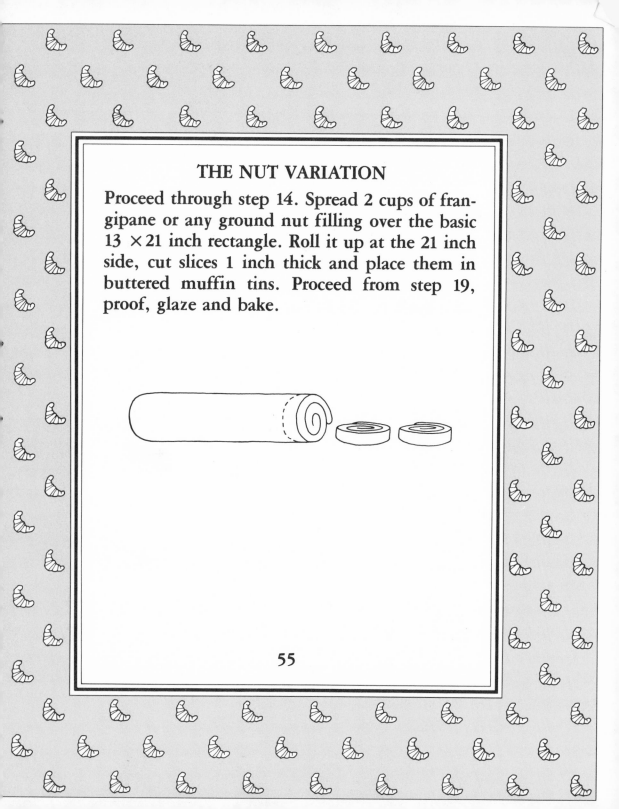

OR

fill with any appropriate, flavorful foodstuff and form into any appropriate, beautiful shape for pastry. Croissant dough may be substituted in any recipe calling for puff pastry or pastry to be deep-fried, and it will add a wonderful yeasty dimension to the flavor. A few more whimsical suggestions...

56

On a Russian Theme:
THE CAVIAR VARIATION

Split a baked croissant and liberally pile on the caviar and sour cream.

On a Norwegian Theme:
THE KIPPER VARIATION

Proceed through step 14. Divide the basic 13×21 inch rectangle into squares about 4×4 inches. Place slices of kippered cod on each square. Fold over on the diagonal, and pinch to seal. Proceed from step 19, proof, glaze and bake.

On an Italian Theme:

THE VITELLO VARIATION

Proceed through step 14. Divide the basic 13 × 21 inch rectangle into squares about 4 × 4 inches. Place ⅓ cup well-seasoned and pre-cooked ground veal on each square. Fold over on the diagonal and pinch to seal. Proceed from step 19, proof, glaze and bake.

On a Grecian Theme:

THE SPANAKOPETA VARIATION

Proceed through step 14. Divide the basic 13 × 21 inch rectangle into squares about 4 × 4 inches. Place ⅓ cup spanakopeta filling on each square. Fold over on the diagonal and pinch to seal. Proceed from step 19, proof, glaze and bake.

On a Sicilian Theme:
THE CALZONE VARIATION

Proceed through step 14. Divide the basic 13 × 21 inch rectangle into squares about 4 × 4 inches. Place ⅓ cup chopped prosciutto, mozzarella and herbs on each square. Fold over on the diagonal and pinch to seal. Proceed from step 19, proof, glaze and bake.

On a German Theme:
THE STRUDEL VARIATION

Proceed through step 14. Divide the basic 13 × 21 inch rectangle into squares about 4 × 4 inches. Place ¼ cup strudel filling on each square. Fold over on the diagonal and pinch to seal. Proceed from step 19, proof, glaze and bake.

On an English Theme:

THE WELLINGTON VARIATION

Substitute croissant dough for the puff pastry in a recipe for Beef Wellington.

On a Scottish Theme:

THE STEAK AND KIDNEY VARIATION

Substitute croissant dough for the puff pastry in a recipe for Steak and Kidney Pie.

DO NOT EXPECT the miracle of the Quintessential Croissant on the first attempt; professional chefs spend years mastering the art. As Rome was not built in a day, only with patience and perseverance will you create the Quintessential Croissant.

Your labors *will* be rewarded. As the beautiful pastry melts away in your mouth, you may experience the Zen moment when nothingness meets eternity.

THE RESPITE OF RESPLENDENT REPAST!